The Ballad of the Long-tailed Rat

by Charlotte Pomerantz • illustrated by Marian Parry

Macmillan Publishing Co., Inc.
New York

Collier Macmillan Publishers
London

10 9 8 7 6 5 4 3 2 1

The three-color illustrations were prepared as pen-and-ink
line drawings with halftone overlays. The typeface is
Alphatype Astro, and the display is Photo Phidian.

Library of Congress Cataloging in Publication Data

Pomerantz, Charlotte.   The ballad of the long-tailed rat.
[1. Rats—Fiction.   2. Stories in rhyme]   I. Parry, Marian, illus.   II. Title.
PZ8.3.P564Bal   [E]   74-13611   ISBN 0-02-774890-1

For Betty and Percy

"**I**'m the landlady
Who saw the cat
Watching the rat

And told the landlord
Who set the trap
With the cheese I bought
Which finally caught
The long-tailed rat.

And that, rat-a-tat, is that, is that.

P.S. It's *my* cat."

"I'm the landlord
Who set the trap,
The big steel trap
That caught the rat.
That dratted cat
Couldn't catch a fly.
No, it was I
Who put cheese in the trap
To catch the rat.

And that, rat-a-tat, is that, is that.

P.S. It's *my* cat."

"You two," sneered the cat,
"Wouldn't even know that
There *was* a rat.
Had the landlady not seen me—the cat—
Waiting, whiffing,
Sniff-sniff-sniffing,
Would the landlord know
Where the rat was at?
Not he nor she would have smelled a rat.

And that, rat-a-tat, is that, is that.

P.S. Nobody *ever* owns a cat."

"It was I, the cheese, who caught the rat.
Not any of you, nor that stinky old cat.
Smooth and creamy with rich butterfat,
I, alone, caught the long-tailed rat.
The rat smelled me, and I smelled a rat.

And that, rat-a-tat, is that, is that.

P.S. Only a fool would count on a cat."

"Clap *trap,* clap *trap,*"
Snapped the voice of the trap.
    pitapat, pitapat
"What's that? What's that?"
    pitapat, pitapat
"Here comes the rat!
I alone caught the long-tailed rat,
Not you, nor that cheese
Nor that fat-head cat.

And that, rat-a-tat, is that, is that.

P.S. Someday I'm going to catch that cat."

"Rattlebrains," squeaked a voice near the trap,
The squeaky voice of the long-tailed rat.
"So what if the landlady saw the cat
Waiting for me, the long-tailed rat,
And told the landlord, who set the trap
With the cheese she bought
Which finally caught—
Or so you thought—
The long-tailed rat.

But it wasn't like that.
No, it wasn't like that!
One whiff of that cheese—
Ugh—I turned and fled,
Which is why my *tail*
Got caught—not my head.

But I'm still a most elegant, long-tailed rat.
A pinch of an inch doesn't change all that.
And that, rat-a-tat, is that, is that.

P.S. Still and all, drat that cat!"